FIONA SAMPSON

the healing word

a practical guide to poetry
and personal development activities

York St John

First published in 1999
by The Poetry Society

Design/layout by Stephen Troussé
at The Poetry Society

All photographs by Haywards, Fisherton Mill, Salisbury,
Wiltshire SP2 7QY

Printed by Grillford Ltd, 26 Peverel Drive, Granby,
Bletchley, Milton Keynes MK1 1QZ

ISBN 1 900771 18 7

Contents

Acknowledgments

The Poetry Society would like to thank Age Concern Swindon and Maura Dooley for permission to reproduce 'Echolalia', Selima Hill for permission to quote from *The Accumulation of Small Acts of Kindness* and *Violet*, Jaan Kaplinski for 'The Sick Body Doesn't Exist' and Pauline Stainer for permission to quote from *The Wound-dresser's Dream*. I would also like to thank these four poets, as well as Robin Downie, Jenny Girvin-Baker, Graham Hartill, Celia Hunt, John Killick, Harriet Klein, Nicki Jackowska and Cheryl Moskowitz for the generosity with which they have discussed their practice.

Finally, we would like to thank all the poets whose work illustrates this guide: especially members of the Greencroft Writing Group, Salisbury, some of whom are published here for the first time, and who chose the section titles.

This Poetry Places project was supported by Southern Arts, Salisbury Health Care NHS Trust and Salisbury Arts Centre.

1 ONCE UPON A TIME

INTRODUCTION

What do we mean by 'poetry and healing'? Do poets write because it makes them feel better? Are there differences between the experiences or needs of writers and readers? What's the point of writing in health care? Any new field has to try to answer fundamental questions of who, where, what, when and especially why. But this guide draws on experience which already exists to look for some answers about poetry and healing.

Making a link between poetry and healing isn't new. In ancient Greece patients in the hospital at Epidaurus would visit not only the sanctuary but also the theatre that formed part of the complex. The Bible has the story of David singing to calm Saul. Chanting forms a part of healing ritual in many cultures.

Poetry anthologies are full of poems of grief, fear, disorientation and loss. Not to mention poetry about reconciliation, joy or desire. Anthologies on themes as varied as bereavement, love and mental distress are highly successful. In fact, one of the most widely held beliefs about poetry is probably that it's first and foremost an expression of emotion.

Ideas Box #1

If you're looking for poems which deal with difficult emotional themes in accessible ways you could try some of these:

Poetry of grief

ed. by Judi Benson and Agneta Falk: *The Long Pale Corridor: Contemporary Poems of Bereavement*; Douglas Dunn: *Elegies*; and Raymond Carver's look at his own death: *A New Path to the Waterfall.*

Poetry of mental distress

Barry MacSweeney: *The Book of Demons*; Anne Sexton ed. by Diane Wood Middlebrook and Diana Hume George: *The Selected Poems*; ed. by Ken Smith and Matthew Sweeney: *Beyond Bedlam.*

About complex relationships

Ted Hughes: *Birthday Letters*; Jackie Kay: *The Adoption Papers.* Her *Off Colour* deals with the sick body.

On illness

The title sequence from Philip Gross: *The Wasting Game*; Thom Gunn: *The Man with Night Sweats*; Susan Wicks: *Singing Underwater.*

Over recent years, though, the idea of a link between poetry and healing has generated a huge amount of activity in therapeutic settings. In the 1970s in the US, Poetry Therapy and

Bibliotherapy – the 'prescription' of discussion texts about experiences similar to patients' own – became popular. The National Association for Poetry Therapy has Certified and Registered Poetry Therapists. However, in the UK since the late 1980's, the practice of facilitating poetry workshops in care settings has emerged out of the Health Care Arts movement. This means that poetry in formal health care is seen here primarily as an arts activity which complements a care setting rather than in the medical model. It's also linked to advocacy – poetry and healing has more to do with individual and active voices than with prescribing what the nature of a patient's experience will be – and this is particularly clear in the increasing number of projects led by the User movement.

Finally, a general cultural shift towards accepting 'talking cures' – including Jungian theories which create scope for the imagination – as well as a fashion for confessional art (for example Women's Art, or the resurgence of publishing interest in autobiography) have led to the development of a market for using writing as self-exploration. That poetry has played a key role in this emerging area of writing and personal development is probably partly to do with the form itself and partly the result of work done by individual poets in the field.

Health Care Arts

The Health Care Arts movement uses professional artists to bring the arts into hospitals, hospice and day and primary care settings not as an 'add-on', or diversion, but in order to humanise the whole delivery of clinical care.

If you'd like to know more about Health Care Arts, a good introduction is: *Helping to Heal*, ed. Peter Senior and Jonathan Croall; *The Arts in Health Care* ed. Charles Kaye and Tony Blee; or *The Arts in Health Care: Learning from experience* ed. Duncan Haldane and Susan Loppert.

As a result, poetry and healing includes a real mixture of styles and activities. This is reflected in the variety of terms we use: 'healing', 'personal development', 'therapeutic', 'care settings'. If you're already confused, try turning to 'Useful Definitions' in section two. Some activities don't sit well together; others seem contradictory. Still others may be bad practice, in terms of providing either a poor literary experience or inadequate care. They may expose people who are feeling vulnerable to inappropriate stress.

One of these apparent contradictions is between the expertise of someone experiencing illness or difficulty (what we call 'vulnerability') or involved in personal development, and that of the professional poet. Another is between institutional processes of health and social care and the individuality which both poetry and healing may promote. Yet poetry now crops up in many of the contexts we turn to when we're vulnerable, ill or at a loss: in private counselling and psychotherapy; NHS, Social Services and voluntary sector care settings; the user movement and self-help activity by individuals and groups. From books and magazines published by Survivor's Poetry Scotland to poetry and personal development weekends at the Indian King Arts Centre in Camelford, from a network of practitioners in Wales to 'poetry washing lines' at Healing Arts: Isle of Wight, there are poetry and healing activities taking place all over the country today.

It's a field in which Britain leads the world. This suggests that:

+ many people in the UK seem to experience poetry as 'relevant' in times of crisis;
+ community, health care and disability arts and access to poetry are overlapping in new ways;
+ we have a major skill resource in the writers and practitioners working in the field;
+ something exciting is going on which formal providers (of the arts and of health and social care) would do well not to ignore.

We'd like to share this excitement and show the kind of activities which can take place, with examples from the best work around. What we won't be doing is trying to prove that poetry cures certain conditions, or that one kind of approach is better than another. But we will be making the case for good practice. We'll suggest ways to set up projects, and try to answer some of the most frequently asked fundamental questions about poetry and healing.

One final note. This book is designed around shared poetry and healing activities because it's important to get things right when we're responsible for enabling other people's experiences. If you are someone who has found writing or reading poetry by yourself healing, we hope that you'll read on and find that you're not alone. We'd like to encourage you to try some of our suggestions for yourself. You might even feel inspired to join or set up a project yourself!

2 UNSCRABBLE THE SCRIBBLE

POETRY AND HEALING ACTIVITIES

The first step is the hardest. If you've never seen poems on the wall of a hospice dayroom, joined a writing club in a group home for people with learning difficulties, or experienced the machismo attached to writing in a psychiatric prison unit, it can be hard to imagine where poetry fits in to a therapeutic setting. Perhaps this is because we either see poetry as too public for the personal dimension in distress, or as too private to share. Poetry and healing, that's to say poetry activities taking place in a therapeutic context, may seem oddly intimate, neither sufficiently formal or informal to match the experience of discomfort.

In fact, though, it's just this mixture of public – poetic form is still sometimes called rhetoric – and private – think how often poetry seems to confess what the narrator is feeling – which seems to make poetry work in the healing context. The shared but intensely personal experience of catharsis which public performance of poetry can generate may be traced back to the origins of tragedy in Greek religious ritual. Nowadays this is often reflected in the reading of a poem at a wedding or funeral: think of W. H. Auden's 'Funeral Blues' in the film *Four Weddings and a Funeral*. Something similar happened at the death of Diana, Princess of Wales, when impromptu shrines of flowers but also of poems were set up in public places. Whether or not those poems were individually memorable isn't so much the point as that there was an *impulse* to poetry.

Useful definitions

The link between poetry and healing has more to do with valuing the individual experience than with an 'expert' taking it over. So how we talk about people and their poetry matters. As far as possible the terms in this guide are in line with current usage.

Clinical practice is the practice of formal medicine. A hospital is a clinical setting but strictly speaking, while a junior doctor is a clinician, a nursing auxiliary is a carer.

We take **personal development** to mean self-examination and development carried out by someone who, whatever their concerns, isn't having sufficient difficulty with everyday life to require formal care. They may or may not be receiving private counselling or therapy.

Therapeutic means offering the individual benefits, whether emotional, physical or spiritual. Thus a support group poetry club may develop confidence, while an arts activity in a hospital might help revive a zest for life. However, clinicians use this term to mean 'relating to therapy'.

Therapy is a practice led by a therapist trained in relevant clinical (i.e. medically diagnosed) conditions as well as in the skills of their profession. Therapies, which include music, art, dance-movement and drama therapy as well as physiotherapy, occupational therapy and psychotherapy, can be clinically prescribed. In other words, they include an initial diagnosis, interpretation in terms of 'symptoms' and a desired outcome.

The therapeutic context means, here, a setting where people are hoping for benefits, either because they're at a vulnerable time in their life or because they're involved in personal development, and which recognises those special needs.

A User is anyone using health or social care. Generally, though, the term is taken up by people whose relationship with care services is sufficiently long-term to become a significant part of their life.

So how is poetry brought into a therapeutic context? Poetry can be written or read. It can be written individually or in groups; it can be read to oneself or aloud. These are the only limits on its use in the context of healing.

Many projects, though, concentrate on shared writing sessions. The poetry writing group requires only a certain amount of quiet and privacy, some paper and pens, and something for participants who're writing to lean on. This makes it cheap, easy to fit round the important clutter of oxygen cylinders or into the confined office-space of a voluntary organisation, and above all flexible. If a medical emergency comes up, a writing group can relocate. If several regular members are unwell, or in an acute unit where everyone is bedbound, sessions can be one-to-one. If a condition such as dyslexia, stroke or a learning difficulty prevents group members from writing down their words, a facilitating poet or other helper can act as a 'secretary'.

Goodbye

It was hard
trying to make you understand
that the journey you'd be taking
was yours alone.

I held your hand.
I felt helpless
struck dumb
mute with fear of
making you frightened.

The machine hummed hypnotic tunes
and the oxygen you sucked on
stretched the days for you;
prolonged the moment of departure.

I thought to pack a bag
to be useful
but there was no need.
You were travelling light.

I tried to explain
how much I loved you
but the words stuck
like a claw in my throat,

I mumbled that I'd miss you
but you didn't hear me.
You were caught between letting go
or holding on tight.

And so we waited
like passengers at a bus stop.
Bus pass and ticket in hand
you stood bravely
trying not to say you didn't want to go.

Sue Moran
(Sue is a member of the Greencroft Writing Group)

On the other hand, poetry is often something unexpected in the therapeutic context. It's newer and more conspicuous than a chat with the social worker. It's more permanent than a conversation with another user at the drop-in. It's more public than a diary and more attractive than a feedback form. It's oblique: it doesn't have to deal with 'issues' and in any case can do so indirectly. It also comes ready-stuffed with everyone's preconceptions about status, education and skill.

Poems, which are visibly language worked into form, get treated with a different order of respect from mere speech. A disproportionate number of prisoners and of people with mental health problems write them; and some gain status because they express shared experiences and through occasional verse (such as poems for birthday cards). Contrary to many carers' expectations, it's not automatically the educated, middle class members of any community who feel most sense of ownership of poetry. This makes sense to anyone who has written out of emotional distress or in private: the process may be many things – a protest, self-exploration, an experiment – but it's unlikely to be led by the idea of 'culture'.

Meanwhile, on the other hand, there are lots of people who have never written a poem before they join a poetry and healing group, and who are unconfident in their ability to do so. After all, what's the definition of successful poetry? Tennyson was so fashionable that he could build a mansion on the proceeds of a single poem. But many important poets of recent decades have gone out of fashion in our own.

In the therapeutic context, someone who attends a session but writes prose, or nonsense, or nothing at all, is as much a participant as the person who turns out to have a wonderful feel for language. In fact, since reading and writing are equally important in the life of a poem, we can say that everyone who joins a poetry session is 'doing' poetry. It's up to their facilitator to make sure that the poetry they're 'doing' is of real quality. In section four we look at the skills he or she needs. Later in this guide, Pauline Stainer and Selima Hill discuss this kind of experience.

There must be as many ways to run a poetry and healing

group as to peel an egg and we're not going to try to itemise them. But we will be looking at ways to add quality (section four) and point out some ethical issues (section six); and if you are thinking about an actual project you'll want to make sure it follows the 'Ten Commandments' of good practice.

The ten commandments

1. Make sure there's supervision (in a health care setting) or at least line management. It's an essential briefing and debriefing support system.

2. Without compromising on quality the experience needs to be accessible. For example, it's unfair to ask people who are heavily medicated for sustained concentration.

3. Exercises and topics should be open-ended enough for people to participate without having to address something they find too difficult.

4. Few if any group members want a writing class. One way to enable really good writing is through first-rate examples and positive feedback.

5. Unless she's being 'secretary' any facilitating poet should take part in writing and discussion in order to reduce the sense that 'real' poetry is somehow withheld or 'other'.

6. Avoid competition!

7. The group's work is confidential, unless everyone agrees otherwise, even when the press want to visit or there's a chance of publication.

8. The chance to express oneself may be, for the individual in a thera-

peutic context, the chance to express difficult emotions and ideas. It's essential that both group leader and participants are clear who is the qualified carer or counsellor to whom they can turn for support if powerful emotions are stirred up. This applies in private settings too: a workshop leader who introduces a demanding topic is responsible if participants are left in a vulnerable state.

9. The facilitating poet's skills, approaches, expectations and exercises are not simply transferable from schools' or other workshop settings.

10. If in doubt, the facilitator should be prepared to ask: participants, clinical professionals or experienced practitioners as appropriate. People who are vulnerable aren't an appropriate group with whom to 'learn on the job'.

Poetry can also be read, of course. With support, families can compile poems as well as messages and other personal readings onto tapes for relatives with visual impairment, in intensive care, or simply too far away for regular visits. Help can take the form of an advice sheet or of a 'tape surgery' session, perhaps at the local Hospital Radio Station, to which families can be referred by unit care staff as part of a support package.

Hospital Radio – and for community based groups local and community radio – is itself an obvious outlet for poetry. Simon Armitage's work on BBC Radio One shows that, even at the busiest end of music-and-talk broadcasting, a poem can 'be heard' as memorable, moving, funny or relevant. Members of established groups may enjoy programming and reading poetry for broadcast as well as broadcasting their own work.

Poetry and healing is an arts activity and it's important to be imaginative when using poetry in the therapeutic environment. Where would you like to see poems? Poem posters are popular nowadays and the public art commissioning budgets of Heath Care Arts projects and Regional Arts Boards make it possible to use poetry in site-specific artworks, including sculpture, inscription, calligraphy and – from tapestries and banners to kneelers for the Hospital chapel – textiles.

Ideas Box #2

Some ways into writing poetry, for groups of people who haven't written before, work especially well.

THEMES

Read two or three poems on a theme together before doing 'open writing' in response. It's a good idea to have copies for everybody and for somebody to read the poems aloud. An easy way in is to discuss the poems one by one in terms of content: do you recognise this emotion? could you tell this was written by a woman? why do you think this poem sounds angrier than the last one?

Example: Larger themes are more useful than particular situations: mothers rather than adoption, belonging rather than ethnicity. They can also generate wider empathy with a particular situation.

Tip: Starting with poems 'ups the stakes' of everyone's imagination.

GAMES

They don't have to be childish. Giving each other starting points creates a sense of ownership of each other's work.

Example: Write down a colour and/or a number, an object of value, anything animal/vegetable/mineral and put your paper in the 'lucky dip' pile or give it to the person on your left to write from.

Tip: Arbitrary starting points and structures can enable unexpected writing: and in a fixed time. Open topics allow individuals to address whatever they want.

WRITING IN FORM

Demystify a form by reading examples together, then make a group poem, then work alone. This works well in a group which has already been building confidence for a few weeks.

Example: Particularly good are haikus and villanelles.

> Round and round goes the Ferris wheel,
> And hearts flutter around that edge of terror
> The clouds sail so nonchalantly by.
> Hands reach up to the dark night sky
> But only heavy summer rain
> Answers their fairground prayer.
>
> [...] Each word of prayer a drop of rain
> Each private terror vast as the sky

> Each heart exhilarated by the perpetual wheel.
>
> From: 'The Gorwelion Six: Sestina' by the Gorwelion Day Hospital Writing Group (with six members).
>
> **Tip**: Take a poetry and healing group as seriously as any other writing workshop.

One way to produce the texts for visual artworks is to run special workshops. Another is to use published poems, for example by subscribing to Poems on the Underground or by selecting poems and obtaining permission to reproduce them.

The selection procedure itself can – and should – involve project participants. A third way to generate appropriate poems is to commission them.

A picture of health

Workshops, primary health care, health education

Dr Malcolm Rigler's waiting room in his GP surgery in Withymoor Village is lively with health education posters which are familiar all over the country. Their striking design and strong slogans belie the fact that they were created in a six-month writing project at the surgery. Poetry they are not, but wide distribution and their role in preventive health care make them exemplary celebrations of the skills of project participants. Also exemplary is the project's active support by a clinician. Without a powerful ally it can be hard for activities to have a long-term, wide impact. Dr Rigler has published widely on this project (see Further Reading).

Commissions, long-stay acute care, the voluntary sector

In 1995 Age Concern Swindon commissioned a set of five poem posters for use in a long-stay hospital. Their aim was 'to provide a human touch and a place for thought for patients, visitors and staff amid the stresses of life in a busy contemporary hospital'. They worked closely with the NHS Trust, especially the hospital's estates manager. Southern Arts' Literature Officer provided funding and support. Poets Fred D'Aguiar, David Constantine, Maura Dooley and Herbert Lomas were each asked to write a poem which 'rather like a proverb' would be accessible but provide the reader with something to think about. The series was completed by a poem from a workshop in one of the wards.

Jo Osorio, Director of Age Concern Swindon, says 'Age Concern organisations are... committed to working for all older people... delivering good quality services [and] applying our experience in new and ingenious ways to meet needs. We aim to make later life a fulfilling and enjoyable experience. The poems for St Margaret's were a straightforward attempt to do just that. Who knows how many people were touched by them as they stopped to have a look – and think? Happily there's lasting pleasure in reading them over again in the booklet we published because now the wards are empty, the hospital is going. The new hospital will have an arts policy. Maybe our influence will show there too'. Age Concern Swindon, who have had a Writing Development Worker since 1992, went on to commission two more poems for Age Concern England's 'Debate of the Age' education and awareness campaign in 1999.

Maura Dooley's poem, 'Echolalia', hangs in the Relatives Room, used for consultations and counselling, at Stratton St Margaret's Hospital:

Echolalia

Her version, her vision,
of the way the world works
is like those lightning moments
when a voice, a face, a street corner
from thirty years ago suddenly recurs,
raw as a cut. You wonder then
if the view is still the same,
the sun just clearing the chimneys
and the trees shape-shifting
all the long afternoon and you know
that it can't be, will always be,
forgetting, for that instant,
which end of the telescope
you're looking through.

Maura Dooley

(collected in *Kissing a Bone*)

3 MAKING SENSE

WHY POETRY AND HEALING?

It's possible to have a private encounter with poetry in times of stress and to bring poetry into therapeutic contexts in lots of imaginative ways. But we need to have reasons to do so. Our reasons for putting poetry in place condition our choices of poetry and the ways we use it.

Let's look at the idea of poetry and healing again. We've seen how using poetry in a therapeutic context means using it in the context of vulnerability or special needs, especially those due to illness or injury, whether you're reading to yourself or coordinating a poetry residency in a day centre. In some of these contexts, 'healing' seems to mean only what clinical and care professionals do. There are no trained poetry therapists, so poetry can't be 'healing' in this sense. There are, though, professional therapists, clinicians and carers who use poetry to 'add value' to their work. There are also professional poets whose work 'adds value' to professional care.

Adding value through poetry in care settings can mean:

+ relaxing participants;
+ getting to know staff and users in different, more personal, fuller ways;
+ making opportunities for enjoyment and interest;

- offering access to skills and affecting the confidence of participants;
- changing who speaks in what can be a disempowering setting, where the individual is just a 'case';
- bringing in new, nonscientific, impractical, flexible ways of thinking and talking.

Added value enables care because it puts staff and clients in a better frame of mind and develops their relationships. Even more significantly, it brings a fuller, humanising dimension into the care setting to inform everything that happens.

Case notes

Professional carers use poetry to add value to their work in a variety of ways.

The psychotherapist

Cheryl Moskowitz is a prose writer and poet as well as a psychodynamic counsellor. A founder member of LAPIDUS, she uses poetry in her counselling work because 'looking closely at disintegrated parts of ourselves and our experience not only opens up vast new [creative] possibilities, but puts us in touch with hidden truths about ourselves and new ways of managing them'. Not all the writing in Cheryl's approach, which she calls 'The Self as Source', is poetry. She encourages participants to create characters who represent different parts of their selves: these characters may then narrate poems.

Cheryl has written about this approach in *The Self on the Page*, edited by Celia Hunt and Fiona Sampson. She also uses her counselling skills to deliver 'Playing with Poetry' sessions in which parent-child 'couples', working together, deepen their relationships as they imagine, think and write together.

The medical ethicist

Since the 1980s a group of clinicians, medical students and academics has met to discuss literature and the human insights it can offer their own practice. Robin Downie, Professor of Moral Philosophy at the University of Glasgow, leads the Glasgow Literature and Medicine Group. He also uses literature when teaching medical ethics to medical students. He says that 'poems... can make a large impact on a student or doctor and develop intuitive understanding'. He makes a distinction between the scientist's 'horizontal' understanding of each experience – say, of an invasive test – as being like many others, and 'vertical' understanding of the 'particularity' of each person's own experience. 'Literature can remind us that what is scientifically typical occurs in unique forms in individual patients.'

Robin collected some of the poetry and prose he uses in *The Healing Arts: An Oxford Illustrated Anthology*.

The occupational therapist

Ceri Davies is Senior Occupational Therapist at an acute mental health care unit. Running a weekly poetry group so interested her that she has also undertaken training at the University of Sussex. Ceri believes strongly in the importance of ethical and practical boundaries to what can be powerful experiences. Her research, in *Occupational Therapy and the Visiting Writer*, an unpublished dissertation for the University, shows

that, significantly, visiting poets are less likely than occupational therapists to value good ethical practice in health care.

Of course the benefits that come with a fuller, more humanised way of working apply to more therapeutic contexts than just formal care settings. They also reflect the aims of holistic complementary health care. They are among the things User groups work towards. And they're reflected in the ultimate person-centered context, where an individual looks after himself, for example by writing poetry in times of stress.

Finally, this approach is reflected in dictionary definitions of healing. According to the *Oxford English Dictionary*, 'healing' is '...restoration to health... mending, reparation; restoration of wholeness, well-being, safety or prosperity; spiritual restoration, salvation'.

The case in point

People who work with poetry outside formal therapeutic contexts report remarkably similar benefits to those identified by professional carers.

The professional poet

    Is there no language
    to localise pain?

Pauline Stainer

(From the title poem of *The Wound-dresser's Dream*)

Pauline Stainer's work often deals with extreme experience, ritual and spirituality. She sees writing poetry as 'all about wholeness and making whole, in the sense of hallowing' experience. She is wary of examining the process which generates her writing too closely, but does 'trust the unconscious' to do what other parts of the mind may find 'inexplicable'.

For Pauline, reading or listening to poetry can also produce a kind of wholeness. She spent some time reading other people's poetry in a hospice and encountered 'a special quality of listening [...] I was never afraid to read poems about death and dying'. Poetry was not an escape from but often 'embraced' the experiences of people who were terminally ill.

The individual writing at home

When a piece on poetry and healing was published in the *British Medical Journal* in 1994 one of the authors, Dr Robin Philipp of Bristol University, was the subject of sixty media reports. These led to unsolicited correspondence not only from 84 health professionals but also from 218 members of the public, 67 of whom sent him examples of their own poetry.

Of the individuals who wrote to Robin from the UK, '42% (83/196) spontaneously reported that reading poetry helped them by incantation of rhythm, silent or aloud, and 42% (82/196) benefited from finding that they could identify with the themes of published poems. Writing poetry was reported by 56% (109/196) to help by providing useful outlet for their emotions'.

This summary, which gives some idea of how important poetry can be in an individual's emotional life, comes from Robin's subsequent letter to *The Lancet*. Robin now plans to set up randomised clinical trials of poetry in health care.

The user movement

Lisa Boardman, Information Worker at Survivors' Poetry, points out that writers receiving mental health care have often had experience of their writing being taken away by clinical staff and as it were 'used against them'. For example it may be read in over-literal terms as a set of symptoms rather than an imaginative product; or the sheer act of producing it may be taken as an indication of 'ill health': introversion, obsessive dwelling on a subject or refusal to participate in group activities. Survivors' Poetry originally grew out of this kind of experience as an advocacy and support network for users of mental health care. Now the organisation has a secure national profile in literature as well as disability arts circles, it has not only begun to widen the possible definition of a survivor (see below) but to be a forum for debate about the relationships between poetry and healing. Some members believe that writing poetry helps them feel better, others that it actually improves their mental health, and still others that it's important to advocate the poetry of people who have been put in a vulnerable position just because that position make them less likely to be able to do so for themselves.

So the idea of poetry and healing includes:

- poetry which goes on in a therapeutic context;
- the ways in which poetry activities may enable other 'healing' activities;

- ways in which poetry can, in any context, create positive feelings and experiences which contribute to 'wholeness'.

A wider definition than this, which couldn't be backed up, would be not only unprofessional – for carers, poets or poetry promoters – but actually dangerous. However much we say and write about special intuitions and sensitivities, being a poet isn't the same as being a therapist. Professional poetry isn't amateur psychology, shamanism or alchemy: though some poets may find elements common to both. Pretended expertise, especially when working with people made vulnerable by an event or illness, is a form of abuse.

Ideas box three

Some poets use themes of alchemy, shamanism and other myths or include "magic" charms:

Meg Bateman: *Lightness and Other Poems*

Robert Graves: *The White Goddess*

ed. by Richard Hamer: 'A Charm' in *A Choice of Anglo-Saxon Verse*

ed. Hofman and Lasdun: *After Ovid: New Metamorphoses*

Ted Hughes: *Winter Pollen: Occasional Prose*

Christopher Logue: *War Music, Kings* or *The Husbands*

George Mackay Brown: *Selected Poems*

Peter Redgrove and Penelope Shuttle: *The Sacred Wound*

Derek Walcott: *Omeros*

Poets who work in therapeutic contexts have to recognise the limits of their powers.

Because it's hard to persuade public funders to back a project which can't be argued for; because as poetry and healing activities have developed some practitioners or providers have wanted to think more deeply about what they're doing; and perhaps because so much activity and enthusiasm involving writers was bound to end in print, research into the nature and effects of poetry and healing activities is going on. Some of this research is anecdotal reportage, some quantitative and some qualitative research.

Project reports on work can be a good source of ideas and examples. They're a form of skill-sharing which is developing the field faster than any other activity at present. There are also several **self-help manuals** for the individual writing alone. Qualitative research uses theoretical disciplines from the humanities – such as education theory, psychoanalysis or literary criticism – to try to explain what happens when people use poetry in a therapeutic context. **Quantitative research**, or the scientific method, aims to identify and measure effects in order to establish a causal connection between poetry activity and identified benefit. Many of the reports, papers and books published look at poetry in the wider field of writing – or artwork in general – in the therapeutic context. You'll find some of the most useful in Further Reading.

A personal story

Poet and novelist Nicki Jackowska's *Write for Life* distils her own personal and professional writing experience and her experience as a writing workshop leader. The book is 'born out of interaction with students' and years of experience of the process of teaching poetry as one of 'joint discovery'. Nicki believes that you can 'gently push and pull on the emotional world in the same way as you can on the technical side'. The book 'asks what happens to us when we use language on the page... it asks what's the difference between simply imagining (for example in guided imagery) and what happens when you start to use language, with the challenges that presents'. *Write for Life* is presented as an imaginative, often playful manual in which the writer draws on their inner resources and the world of their experience; but it also suggests that by bringing experiences and ideas into the medium of language we change them. Some of the experiences Nicki uses as examples are her own and are painful to read. Writing allows us to work on the chaos of experience and 'is essential in the upholding of our humanity, because if we don't have it we go into the undifferentiated area: [writing] is a differentiating tool'. For Nicki, then, writing is the start of ethics, of reparation and of healing. She's now working on a book about Jung and the recovery of lost worlds.

Of course there's a qualitative element – of research led by ideas rather than evidence – in every investigation. Even quantitative research has to decide what to compute. Will it count the number of times respondents mention how reassuring they find formal metre, or how many rhyming rather than free verse lines have been memorised? Some people may feel that to read poetry in this way is reductive. Others worry that to have scientists speak for poetry, or for the individuals who write those poems, is to reinforce the problematic paradigm in which the clinician knows the layman better than he does himself. Still other practitioners may feel that it is the work of creating access to exciting writing practice which is important, rather than reflection which they fear is overly academic.

On the other hand, care professionals who do get involved in poetry and healing activities may feel compromised if they can't advocate the practice using terms their profession recognises. They may wonder why practitioners avoid 'proper' scrutiny.

These concerns reflect the difficulty of defining a new field and of deciding who's qualified to practice in, let alone speak for, it. Is the use of poetry in therapeutic contexts really arts work, a political activity, or a care science? It's not primarily trying to produce professional writers but neither is most literary activity, whether public readings, residency workshops or the marketing of books. Its scope is marked out by its context but so is the content of a school's workshop or a commercial literary festival event. It may affect local social perceptions of poetry or of the project's participants: so does a residency in a High Street store or a poetry slam. On the other hand, without real poetry expertise it can be nothing more than a social activity, encounter group or an exercise in language skills. In other words poetry and healing activities are primarily poetry experiences and depend on a high quality poetry input to work.

The autobiographical eye

Three poets whose autobiographical prose explores the ways their experiences inform and even generate their writing:

Lauris Edmond, the New Zealand poet whose three volume *An Autobiography* made her a spokesperson for women of her generation and the ways they have found to write;

Janet Frame, New Zealand novelist and poet whose three-volume *An Autobiography*, which was made into the film *An Angel at my Table*, records how she was rescued from compulsory hospitalisation by the publication of her poetry;

May Sarton, American poet and woman of letters, who examines her life and writing practice in *Journal of a Solitude*.

One of the best ways to join in, find out more, and come across reports on activities in the field is to attend conferences. Dedicated conferences are rare, but the field is touched on under topics as diverse as reminiscence, writing in education, health care arts, autobiography and women's writing. Many of these are run by organisations, such as the National Association of Writers in Education, Arts for Health or Age Exchange, whose interests similarly overlap with the field. There are also two dedicated national organisations.

LAPIDUS, the Association for the Literary Arts and Personal Development, was formed out of a Poetry Society Special Interest Group in 1996. It has over 120 members, who receive a quarterly newsletter and can attend conferences and local meetings. It's run by a voluntary committee. Branches in Brighton, London and Scotland have programmes of presentations and workshops. LAPIDUS is designed to raise awareness of writing and personal development, and to be a co-ordinating agency for individuals and initiatives in the field. You can contact LAPIDUS at: Box Tree Cottage, Kingswood Road, Hillesley, Wotton under Edge, Gloucestershire GL12 7RB.

Survivors' Poetry was formed in 1991 to celebrate the talents of survivors: 'a person with a current or past experience of psychiatric hospitals, a recipient of ECT, tranquillisers or other medication, a user of counselling services, a survivor of sexual abuse, child abuse and any other person who has empathy with the experiences of survivors'. There are currently thirteen groups around the country, from Aberystwyth to Essex, and more are starting up. The performance of poetry by survivors is central to their work of bringing new voices forward. They also run workshops and festivals, set up exhibitions and publish a quarterly newsletter. Survivors' Poetry can be contacted at Diorama Arts Centre, 34 Osnaburgh Street, London NW1 3ND.

Grouping together

It's worth thinking about forming your own group of like-minded people. Poets Graham Hartill and Angela Morton set up Alembic by invitation. Both work with poetry and personal development and the dozen or so members of their group include users, practitioners and poets with little experience but masses of interest. They meet three times a year, in Abergavenny, for a day of discussion and presentations. Because the group's comparatively small and informal, and because it's closed, members can take risks and develop new ideas in their discussions. They also avoid time-wasting formal administration.

4 FOR WHAT IT'S WORTH

ADDING QUALITY

If a high-quality poetic experience is an essential part of poetry and healing, are poets the experts to deliver that experience? What do poets know about poetry that other professionals – such as literary critics or playwrights – don't?

Haiku

Autumn leaves dancing,
dying in a breath, like you.
Skeleton branches.

Sue Moran

The one thing that unites poets – those with academic backgrounds and performance poets, members of all cultural traditions, poets who are blocked and those writing well – is an especial interest and enthusiasm, some sort of feeling for the capacities of, poetry. If poetry is a mixture of the measurable and the immeasurable, craft and flair, words and what informs them, a professional poet's own relationship with the form will already be made up of all of these elements.

A poet can:

- enthuse;
- demystify poetry both through their actual presence and in their responses to poems;
- share their own working practices;
- give a sense of access to and participation in poetry itself rather than of some dilute, downgraded or secondhand activity.

Of course, not all poets have the personality for work in a therapeutic context. A patronising or inflexible attitude doesn't encourage poetic activity in any context!

Friendliness, on the other hand, can make even a distinguished international poet accessible. And it's important to remember that there are exceptional cases where poetry is delivered very well in the therapeutic context by professional carers or group members who have a particular interest in and knowledge of the field.

Things to translate

In 1997 Piotr Sommer was poet in residence at Aberystwyth International Poetryfest. During that time he led sessions at two day hospitals. The community workshop is unknown in Poland, where Piotr works as a poet and literary translator and edits the bestselling *Literature in Translation*.

Nevertheless, he and a group of users talked about his life under communist rule and after, and about the poems he read. He read in both Polish and English. At Hafan Hedd, in Newcastle Emlyn, a user read and then translated a Welsh poem on the wall in a formal gesture of poetic exchange.

The poems Piotr read were from his collection in English, *Things to Translate*.

However, every project needs a leader who is responsible for adding quality to a project. Poetic expertise is essential here too. Though any project should think in terms of special events and outcomes from the outset, it needs to be characterised throughout by good practice. Here are some key do's and don'ts:

1. Quantity isn't quality. A well-supported group of three or four participants may have a more valuable experience than thirty frail older people who've been brought into a day room for a reading some of them can't even hear.

2. Present and keep presenting your project in the ways you, the participants, see it. Non-participating care staff, relatives or members of the public may have pronounced expectations – not always positive and sometimes subtly reductive – about a community poetry project.

3. Not all the poetry in a project should reflect a facilitating poet's own style.

4. The balance between process and product is important not because process is somehow 'healing' in a way that producing a finished poem isn't, but because it's in enabling the process that a workshop leader enables the product. Getting the balance between process and product right means, for example,

not editing participants' poems without their consent.

5. Working with poetry should never be routine.

Meanwhile, special events can take many forms. They may include add-ons, special occasions which are in addition to core activities, Russian doll projects – special projects within a project – or collaborative programming, involving the expertise of another agency.

Ideas box #4

Add-ons

1. Visiting a literature event or play.
2. Arranging library provision for residents of a nursing home.
3. Commissioning a textile artist to work with poetry on a banner for your venue.
4. A visit or mini-residency by another poet.

Russian doll projects

1. A series of themed workshops or activities (perhaps cross-arts) within a residency.
2. Work towards particular outcomes, for example a group reading on local radio or a publication, in the middle of a project.
3. Exchanges between the groups participating in a project.

Collaborative programming

1. Exchanges with other community groups e.g. between two community art groups in different parts of the country, or between a group of schoolchildren and a community of older people.

2. Participation as performers or programmers in events such as a regional literature festival.

3. Winning a commission from another agency, for example a community newspaper or a local playbus scheme.

A project leader – whether a facilitating poet or a group member – is always responsible for something more than just a series of workshops. Every project activity needs to be thought out, with an end point, themes and structures which will make it safe, enjoyable and accessible.

Good project outcomes add quality to all these activities. There are two kinds of outcome: the satisfaction of aims and objectives (a process of evaluation and feedback) and – probably satisfying at least one of those objectives – the creative products which are the project's legacy. Aims and objectives give a project integrity. But evaluation needs to be carefully done. For example, how do you approach people who have left a group for feedback?

Haiku

When winter snows melt
Spring snowfall drifts down soft pink.
But petals don't melt.

Jan Alford
(Jan is a member of KickStart Poets and
of the Greencroft Writing Group.)

Creative outcomes can't be manipulated so easily. But they represent much more than just accountability. They are part of each participant's personal engagement with poetry.

They may include works of literary merit. If every poet writes for an ideal reader, poetry and healing project participants need access to a readership at some point in order to have the full experience of writing. But this doesn't mean rushing towards publication as a goal. It may mean establishing poetry penfriend twinnings between user groups or commissioning a designer to create poem posters from work. Above all, though, it should avoid the poorly laid-out pamphlet of poems which excludes any audience except next of kin!

Ideas box #5

These showcase ideas could work for groups or individuals.

Performance: If everyone is well enough, why not have a roadshow to community venues? Performance creates a sense of special occasion and using a microphone and other special equipment can be fun.

Poem postcards and greetings cards: Poems on mugs, mats and town maps. If they raise money for the group that's all the more empowering.

An exchange between writing groups is like publication, meeting the critic and acquiring instant likeminded friends all in one.

Making an exhibition of yourself needn't be embarrassing. It could be as creative as designing a display for a local library or collaborating with the Embroiderers' Guild.

It's important for a leader to know what they're doing. That can be hard to establish in a field where there's no training. Experience counts. But sharing roles is probably the best way to bring experience in. The arts administrator has experience of running projects but doesn't know much about disability issues or poetry. The professional poet hasn't worked in health care before but does have experience of working in prison and personal experience of health issues. The self-help group doesn't include any professional poets but there's lots of project experience and clarity about health issues. It doesn't matter how these things are arranged so long as i) the three key areas of expertise – poetry, project management and therapeutic context issues – are properly covered and ii) the facilitating poet has expertise in both poetry and therapeutic context issues.

Haiku

The blossoms fall on
to the ground where a child runs
in the summer sun.

Ann Smith
(Ann is a member of the Greencroft Writing Group.)

For the poet who wants to work in poetry and healing there are several ways in:

- shadow an experienced practitioner;
- volunteer or work in hospital radio, the local hospice, or care work;
- undertake training.

For groups and organisations wanting to develop a project there are also several alternatives:

- bring an experienced practitioner in as a 'consultant';
- hire an experienced practitioner to lead the project;
- go to a reputable organisation, such as the Poetry Society or a Regional Arts Board, and ask them to help identify an experienced practitioner and plan the project.

The field of experienced practitioners, administrators and indeed project users is growing fast at the moment. It probably needs to offer:

- a register of experienced practitioners;
- a consultancy service;
- a recognised training course.

The case for training

In 1996 Dr Celia Hunt set up the Post-Graduate Diploma in Creative Writing and Personal Development at the University of Sussex. Celia became interested in the field as a result of teaching creative writing and autobiography in the university. She wanted to 'encourage people to reflect on their practice', using theory but also exposing what they were doing and thinking about to 'rigorous discussion'. Celia says, 'Unless you create an environment where these discussions can take place they may not happen'. Just over a dozen writers, teachers, counsellors and health care professionals graduate each year. The course covers issues of practice and principle and all students work on their own writing in a personal development context.

5 RIGHT HERE, RIGHT NOW

A WHERE AND WHEN OF PROJECTS

Different kinds of poetry activities are appropriate for different settings: previous sections have suggested the range of possibilities. This section concentrates on four models. Because the mixture of skills and expectations different participants bring to a project is so significant, we look at these examples from a variety of standpoints.

1. Playing in the house of ages

The carer

John Killick is a poet who has worked with over four hundred people suffering from dementia since 1994. He is writer-in-residence for Westminster Health Care. Helen Finch is a carer looking after her mother, who is suffering from dementia. She read about John Killick's work in the Alzheimer's Disease Society Newsletter:

> [...] It seemed to offer some hope. When, at my invitation, John worked with her in the nursing home I was tremendously impressed by how much Eve was able to express to him, even on the first of their four meetings. She was able, despite the severity of her speech impairment, to talk both

widely and deeply and to vouchsafe to him things which she might not have done to me. He was able to give her space and time, and by concentrating intently on what she said and writing it down, he established a rapport very quickly. I believe she recognised instinctively that he valued her for herself. To quote from the poem John made from her speech:

> The past... I think a lot about it...
> I'm thinking when... I'm not saying anything...
> It's silverly, perfectly silverly.

The first two lines embody an important perception, and in the last I believe she is referring to John himself, defining in a symbolic way some of his qualities. In another verse Eve says:

> Anyway, it was a real life, I think.
> Here, now, life takes its... you know.
> I don't think there's anything else.

She took John aside to confide these thoughts, which are reassuringly consistent with the philosophy she held all her life: that of living for the moment.

> I realised that here was someone reaching out directly (his phrase [is] 'communicating as if your

life depended on it') to people with dementia: it was like a ray of light and helped diffuse my negative feelings. He enabled me to feel more confident about the possibility not only of preserving but of strengthening my relationship with my mother.

Some of John's thoughts about links between the writing and the person are explored in *Writing for Self-Discovery*, with Myra Schneider.

2. Three up

The experienced practitioner

Healing Arts: Isle of Wight may hold the record for the longest writing residency in health care. Three writers have occupied the post since it was created in 1988. Originally set up to work throughout a District Health Authority, the project resumed in 1992 – after a three year gap – concentrating work in the areas of community care and mental health which had proved most successful. Harriet Klein, who took up the post from 1994-9, found 'there were definite advantages to such a long residency. For people with long term health problems it was particularly helpful. I got to know people very well and watched their writing and their confidence develop'. The idea isn't to produce a writing dependency culture, though: 'at least one of the groups hopes to run independently now' and Harriet sees her role as enabling participants' own processes: 'When people found their 'voice' through writing, I was able to ensure it was heard'. She did this by working with participants on the literary quality of their writing, as well as through a programme of writers' visits and special events including 'public performances, exhibitions, greetings cards, poetry videos and various installations such as the floating of a poem on the hospital pond'. The unusual link between public art and participating writing groups is one of the things which especially characterises Harriet's residency. Her successor may well work differently. This long-running residency allows us to understand how significant the individual enthusiasms and strengths of a poet in residence are for the whole shape of a project.

3. *I write poetry to tell you / how I feel*

The user

Why I write poetry

You ask me why
I always question.
Poetry is expression,
Feelings moulded into words,
Shaped into sentences.
 A transient feeling

Encapsulated into words
Set free from the mind
That today feels
Anger, hatred, sadness, joy.

Set down on paper.
Written by hand
Typed by fingers:
I write poetry to tell you
How I feel – but do you listen?

Jenny Girvin-Baker's poems have been published in a series of professionally designed poem posters, performed, exhibited and read on BBC Radio Four. In 1992 she joined the writing group at her local Day Hospital because she had enjoyed English and writing at school and college, although she was unsure whether she would be able to write poetry. 'Well from early 1993 I have not really stopped. I found I could use poetry as a release valve for my feelings and this helped my recovery after my breakdown then and in 1998.'

Although she participated in sessions over two years, Jenny developed a poetic voice quite early in the project. 'In the group as well as studying different poems and their styles we would try exercises such as Triolets and Haiku or word games. I would sometimes find these restrictive, but one particular style I found that I did enjoy was the acrostic, where I would pick a particular word or phrase and work out what

I wanted to say by using the initial letter on each line.

'One of the highlights for me was when one of my early poems, 'Time', was made into a Poem Poster [...]. The launch was an invitation-only event and was held in the library. One of my ex-husband's bosses was there representing the Cultural Services Department. He had always just known me as the wife of one of his employees and although he knew I was divorced did not know that I had changed my surname. He came over and asked me what I was doing at this event as he hadn't seen my name anywhere. Who was I representing? It gave me a really good feeling to tell him Me, I was there in my own right as an exhibitor. It seemed to me that at last I could be recognised as my own person and not just as a part of someone else.

'Another highlight was being part of a group that was recorded for a programme on Radio Four. I had to read one of my poems and explain why I had written it. Again the poem, 'Looking and Seeing', was an expression of my feelings at the time [...]. I [...] was so surprised when my voice opened the programme and even more so when people who I didn't think would even listen to Radio Four came up to me and said they had heard me.'

Jenny's most recent poems are called 'Black Poems from even Blacker Days'. After a weekend leave, 'I was back in hospital on the Monday and taking them to show the Occupational Therapist when I was called in to see the Consultant Psychiatrist. We talked and I felt he was still missing the point I was trying to make so I handed him the poems and suggested he should read them and hopefully he would realise how depressed I was. He glanced over them but instead of commenting on the feelings expressed in them he admired the presentation. Later that day in the Creative Writing Group I wrote a poem expressing my feelings about him!' On the other hand, the same poems are being used in a support group 'to show other depressed people they are not alone in how they are feeling'.

Like many people who start in a group but go on to write alone, Jenny is faced with the question of what to do next. 'It has been good to look back and see how I have progressed both with the depression and my poetry writing. I'm glad I joined the group, however, as it has shown me what I am capable of. As to the future, maybe I will join another group, or try to get some of my work published.'

4. *I watch for her until she's really there*

The professional poet

> A blossom fills the lawns of scented gardens,
> fluttering whispers fill the patient's throat.
> Love is more than simple acts of kindness:
> it comes from deep within us like a note.

Selima Hill
(From *The Accumulation of Small Acts of Kindness*)

Selima Hill talks of wanting to share with others 'a sort of messianic zeal' about the experience of writing. She has a 'sense of joy, gratitude and relief at being a writer'; but sees being a writer not as an exclusive professional preserve but as the correct term for anyone who's doing writing. 'Not: a poet is a special kind of person, but: each person is a special kind of poet.'

Her own experience of writing poetry is 'redemptive... transforming the chaos of distress into order... offering myself back to myself and to others... getting stuff hidden inside out onto the page'. But Selima fights shy of the fashionable term 'therapy'. She also plays down her own writing in workshop settings and instead emphasises participants' own abilities and power: 'No-one gives you the power: you just take it!'.

If each writer is central to their own writing, writing poetry – whether in groups, alone or for publication – is partly a form of self-acceptance: 'Take yourself as you find yourself and start from that. Write as you can and do not try to write as you can't. The person you are is much nicer than the person you think you ought to be'. A piece first published in *The Rialto* magazine, 'Selima Hill on Selima Hill: Why I Write Poems', is a list not of aspirations but of sources for poems. These sources are the poet's own experiences, of both feelings and events. Such sources may include a writer's own mental distress.

Although Selima enjoys 'the fellowship of writer[s] and

readers', she identifies the experience of the writing process as a real reward. This experience, of poetry as 'an attitude of attention – a way of life', can be shared by new writers and much-published professionals alike. Poetry is, after all, not a peculiar medicine for special people but something altogether more inclusive and generous: 'Poetry as prayer'.

Many of Selima Hill's collections of poetry deal with specific emotional experiences: see Further Reading. The title of this section is from the first line of *Violet*.

6THE WRITE WAY?

THINKING ABOUT ETHICS

What have ethics got to do with creativity? If we work with ethics are we working too closely with the very health and social care professions whose work we may complement or even challenge but should not imitate? Is it dangerous to over-regulate an activity which seems, to newcomers at least, to be in its infancy? Can't teachers just stir up the creative juices of their students? What do I do if the star poet in our group won't let their poems be read on our great new local radio slot? How do you stop gossip – isn't it just human nature?

Ethics

Ethics are generally defined as having something to do with practice:

> The Ethicke and Politic consideration, with the aim of well doo-ing and not of well knowing onely.
>
> Sir Philip Sidney in *Apologia Poetrie*

> The science of morals; the department of study concerned with the principles of human duty [...] the rules of conduct recognised in certain associations or departments of human life.
>
> *The Oxford English Dictionary*

Professionals working in a therapeutic context have codes of ethics and practice. This is partly to define their practice but also to protect themselves and the people they work with. Arts professions don't have codes of ethics, though they work within health and safety codes and legislation. These protect the member of the public who is in an arts organisation's hands from, for example, food poisoning and fire hazard. But an individual's emotional or mental health is equally significant. We need to remember that activities such as workshops, in which a participant might reveal part of their sense of self, carry with them a risk of emotional harm. This is especially true in a therapeutic context, where a participant is already vulnerable.

Another way to say this is that people who take part in poetry and healing activities need their basic rights – including the right not to be harmed – respected as they should be anywhere. This is especially true if 'healing' includes the idea of enhancing a fuller way of being.

Though therapists who use poetry in their professional practice already have codes to follow, poets working in a therapeutic context don't. They must borrow their ethics. One way to do this is to work within the ethical code of the care unit or organisation in which a project is based. In fact not to do so is, in a deep sense, to refuse to work in the therapeutic context. For that context isn't a building but a set of practices on which the individual who finds himself there must be able to count. He becomes vulnerable if any one team member moves away from them. For example, it only takes one person to break confidentiality.

It's generally the code not of ethics but of practice which varies from unit to unit in health or social care. For example, the arrangements for supervision in psychotherapy-based mental health care – a formal periodic debriefing with a named line manager – differ from the practice of 'hand-over' on a residential/inpatient health or social care unit, in which outgoing and incoming shift teams run over the events of the previous hours together.

A fit body doesn't exist

The Estonian poet and Nobel nominee Jaan Kaplinski writes repeatedly about experience itself, including the experience of making the very poem he's writing. His vision of living as process includes an interest in the process of writing. Discussing some early poems, he says 'They seem to come from another life, written by a very different person, although often at the same table here in the attic room. Our surroundings keep us together, our tables, walls, paths and shelves are the banks between which we are flowing, becoming. Once I wrote that what we call ourselves is really becoming ourselves, a process like burning. Even our memory is not a safe where everything is kept, but taking something out from there is a process, a new becoming too, and using our memory we in reality change it, remould it...'

> A fit body doesn't exist. There are only space,
> extension, endless possibilities,

the fact that you can touch that birch tree there,

fetch the big white stone from the ditch.

The sick body is everywhere: the room, courtyard,

path to the well, the house and the pale-blue sky

are all full of it. The sick body

is so big that everything touches,

hurts and injures it. A spruce branch swaying

at the fence comes in and bruises your face.

The wind swinging in the witches' broom

blows through your breast.

The swallows' cries hit you like hammer blows.

Night falls like an old wet blanket on your eyes and mouth.

Jaan Kaplinski

(From *Summers and Springs*)

Some practitioners worry about working in ways which echo how professional care is organised. They're anxious about an imbalance of power or lack of spontaneity. But it's important to remember that codes of ethics and practice protect the rights of participants rather than encroach further on them.

However some projects take place in a context where there's no developed code. For example, you may set up a writing group for fellow sufferers from Post Natal Syndrome; or decide to run residential 'poetry and personal development' courses in your idyllic Borders farmhouse. But all work with people needs to protect their rights to what the British Association for Counselling's Code of Ethics and

Practice calls 'safety and privacy'. No one can reinvent the whole field of ethical practice by themselves. So it's important to borrow a code such as the BAC's where there isn't one already in place.

Several guides to community arts or residency practice overlap with the field of poetry and healing. Some of these suggest ethical guidelines. 'Further Reading' has details.

Whichever code you borrow, you need to make sure it covers six key areas:

1. **Confidentiality**. Unless otherwise agreed, nothing spoken or written in the session, nor any other information gleaned as a result of the work, for example in supervision, goes any further.
2. **Competence**. No-one involved claims professional skills she or he does not have.
3. **Accountability**. Agreement on who makes major practical or ethical decisions about the project, and how, whom and what they consult.
4. **Responsibility**. Clarity about the roles of everyone concerned and how they interact with each other and the wider community.
5. **Clarity about boundaries**. Not only professional roles but the project and the practice in general have limits which need to be defined and observed.
6. **Participant autonomy**. Even someone who is receiving compulsory health care has the right to intellectual and creative autonomy.

You also need to think through the special challenges of writing in the therapeutic context. Here are a few:

* ownership of intellectual copyright:
    i) storage (who keeps a record?)
    ii) why photocopy if it's confidential?
* artistic merit:
    i) editing/altering texts (why?)
    ii) who is supposed to know what is a good poem?
* publication:
    i) written permission procedures
    ii) appropriate forms and forums (when is someone's work being used as an example rather than treated like a poem?)
* privacy versus publicity and research:
    i) permission and persuasion
    ii) the media e.g. press photos.

Though the code you chose may technically be voluntary it's vital to follow it rigorously, as it's a contract with everybody taking part in your activity.

On the other hand, if you're interested in joining a poetry group working in a therapeutic context but don't know what kind of experience it will offer, you can check:

1. Is at least one reputable not-for-profit organisation involved, or has the facilitator had extensive experience with such a

body? They are likely to be careful about the kinds of practice they support.

2. Which code of ethical practice is the project following? If it has its own, can you see a copy?

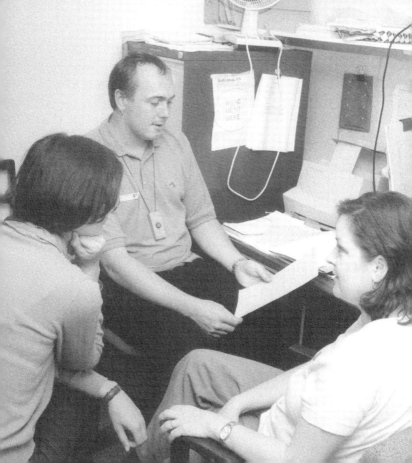

7 DON'T FORGET THE SMALL PRINT

SETTING UP A PROJECT

This book was prepared as part of a Poetry Place working in *Salisbury Health Care NHS Trust*. In this section we use the residency to look at ways to organise a poetry and healing project. If you're already involved in a project, we hope it gives you new ideas. If you'd like to start something up, we hope it will encourage you to move ahead. If you write or read poetry alone we hope you'll find inspiration for future partners and activities.

1. The idea

It all starts with an idea, by which we mean more than just a general interest. An idea is backed up either by some sort of experience, whether organisational (you're an arts organisation used to running community residencies) or personal (you are a social worker with experience of group-work); expertise (you are a professional poet) or knowledge (you're running a community arts project and have identified the market for writing).

In other words the idea has some structure. You may think of a collaboration between two providers; or a project culminating on National Poetry Day; or know of an experienced practitioner and a day centre keen to be involved in arts work who would go well together. The Salisbury project happened because four organisations had overlapping ideas at similar times.

The Poetry Society had the idea of a publication about poetry and healing because of the growth of interest in a field in which it's been involved over the years. Southern Arts wanted to run a high-quality model health care residency to move their contribution on from the major project they instigated in 1988 (see 'Three Up' in section five).

Salisbury Arts Centre had run a pilot project with Salisbury Health Care NHS Trust the previous year. A local poetry club, *KickStart Poets*, attended poet Graham Hartill's workshops in community care settings which led to a poetry event on World Mental Health Day. The Centre wanted to build on the success of this work.

Salisbury Health Care NHS Trust has a developed programme of arts provision across genres and settings. Emma Ryder Richardson, the ArtsCare Manager, was keen to develop writing and literature activities and approached the Arts Centre about collaborating first on the pilot and then on a longer programme.

Having worked continuously in writing and health care for eleven years, *the practitioner* wanted to do more than simply make something interesting happen with and for the particular individuals she met. She wanted to connect this practice with her own and other people's thoughts about the field in general. These agendas helped give Kingfisher Project its shape.

Hampshire

I used to live in Buckinghamshire,
Hazlemere.
Not the one in Surrey
the one in Buckinghamshire.
They say Beechy Bucks
because it's known for a lot of beech trees,
Buckingham is Burnham Beeches.

But I've liked Hampshire,
it's nice country.
It's all farms, lots of animals
and nice country.
It's not so similar to Buckingham because
it hasn't got a lot of beech trees.
It's got oak trees – I likes the oak trees -
sycamore trees, elm trees or ash.
Hornbeams.

Oh yes, I like spending my time outdoors.

Philip Tucker
(Philip, who has a learning difficulty,
was being treated on Amesbury Orthopaedic
Ward at Salisbury District Hospital.)

2. Planning

Though the process may involve a whole sequence of meetings, eight areas are of the essence in planning a project. They are:

1. Agreeing aims. Who is being enabled and why? How will this project add value to on-going activities?

   At Salisbury, the project's aims were to produce a general guide advocating the field, and to create from scratch a programme of literature activities for people using the range of Salisbury Health Care NHS Trust facilities.

2. Consulting for expertise: finding out from the poet, other team members and other professionals likely to be involved (such as clinicians) what kinds of activity may work and which they're prepared to experiment with.

   The Salisbury Poetry Place evolved from a pilot project which the practitioner helped the Arts Centre and ArtsCare to design. It also came out of many discussions between the Poetry Society and practitioners. Liaison with care units was carried out by the Trust's ArtsCare Manager.

3. Identifying specific contexts for proposed activities. See 4) below.

4. Budgeting: how much will proposed activities cost? how much is in the budget up-front? what money needs to be raised and by whom?

Some likely costs

The practitioner
- A practitioner should be paid at least £150 a day (in 1999).
- For short-term projects with long-distance writers, add travel and subsistence costs.
- Most practitioners are self-employed, which means that they are Schedule D tax payers. Although they can claim back PAYE Income Tax, repayment comes much later than the end of the current financial year, and National Insurance contributions are neither reclaimable nor do they add to the practitioner's self-employed contributions.

Running costs
- Management fees buy time so a project can be properly run.
- Room hire fees, stationery, photocopying and tea and coffee for participants are all significant in facilitating a project and need to be planned ahead.

Special events
- Allow £500 for equipment, printing costs and venue hire for special 'showings' such as publications or performances in a six-month project, even though at this stage you may not know what form they will take. If you plan to collaborate with visual artists and/or designers, for example in the production of commercial poem-posters or banners, you will need a much larger budget.
- Visiting writers need fees and expenses and there may be hospital-

ity and room hire costs too.

---

5.   Identifying sources of funding. Your regional arts board is a good source of information as well as a potential funder. Be aware that:

* a potential funder is a potential partner. For example, the Borough Council may be able to fund activities which meet their own criteria. This might add a whole new programme to your project.
* it doesn't matter what level of funding you achieve, so long as your proposals are appropriate. What doesn't work is to ask local amateur groups to 'make up' professional provision; or to go ahead as if unsecured funding will arrive and then stop the project half-way through.
  The Kingfisher Project in Salisbury is funded by The Poetry Society, Southern Arts, Salisbury Health Care NHS Trust and Salisbury Arts Centre.

6.   Formalising the link between budgets and proposed activities through:

  i)   objectives: a programme of activities and their end-points;
  ii) an itemised budget. Objectives need detailed input and consent from venues and practitioner. The budget should be agreed in detail by the practitioner and all project partners.

In Salisbury some workshop projects have a three-month projected life-span but others run for longer. Permissions procedures, approved by the NHS Trust's Ethics Committee, are built into the objectives, as are feed-back and evaluation, commissions, and performances by participants. The practitioner works within the ethical code of each care unit.

7. Finding a project steering group. All project partners should be represented by named individuals. This steering group has responsibility for managing project and practitioner, often by allocating areas of responsibility, and will meet regularly throughout the project.

   The Salisbury steering group meets roughly every six weeks. Meetings are attended by the practitioner. The members are: Keiran Phelan, Southern Arts; Jill Low, Director and Catherine Sandbrook, Manager, Salisbury Arts Centre; Emma Ryder Richardson, Manager, ArtsCare at Salisbury Health Care NHS Trust; Roland Challis, Chair, KickStart Poets.

8. Agreeing a timetable. This will include:
   - start-up meetings (staff training, induction, 'taster' days);
   - frequency, length, time and dates of regular sessions;
   - arrangements for practitioner leave or sickness;
   - planning, run-in and delivery dates for special events where planned and/or approximate areas and timescales for such events;

- dates and desired outcomes for the end of the project (with contingency plans for continuation where appropriate).

3. Managing the project

Though an experienced practitioner probably needs little input, good management frees up practitioner time and allows her to spend her energies on creative strategies rather than strategies of persuasion with under-briefed staff or participants. It may be easiest to have one partner in the steering group acting as 'line manager' for the practitioner.

Try to support the delivery of workshops as well as special events. If the practitioner is skilled these will be exciting, generating the engagement – and writing – which special events ride on. Knowing what's really going on helps you plan and advocate.

The Salisbury project backs up six-weekly steering group meetings with line management through the ArtsCare Manager – who understands the concerns of NHS managers and carers – and the Arts Centre Manager, who is experienced in running residencies.

Initial planning decisions are refreshed by rolling evaluation and feedback, including monthly feedback forms in groups, a session diary by the practitioner, a photocopied record of writing where permission is given and access to other forms of feedback such as a performance on World Mental Health Day and photography.

Untitled

A blank page MUST be filled.
It's a compulsion.
Put down something,
Anything,
Then pause.
A fallow moment.

I see a garden pot
Waiting to be turned over,
A forkful at a time.
How long it takes
Depends much on the soil:
Whether there's loam
Beneath the weeds,
Or stones, or builders' rubble.

Nothing can grow
Until the earth is turned.
Planting must wait
Until the plot is cleared.

It's hard labour.
Back-breaking.
Mind-breaking
Sometimes.

But then sun warms the soil
A robin comes to feed
On new-mined worms;
A wildflower offers up
Its gentle scent;
A bird sings after rain.

One sense wakens another,
raking up memories.
The words arrange themselves,
The plot's revealed.

Jan Alford

4. The groups

Criteria for selecting groups are simple. They must want to work with the project. They need an enthusiastic worker or volunteer to coordinate their group. Their timetables must work alright. It's good to have a range of types of unit in a project.

The Kingfisher Project involves four groups who meet fortnightly and a fifth involved in occasional events.

The Greencroft Centre is a drop-in facility which supports people with longer-term mental health problems who live in the community. The writing group, with attendances of between five and eleven, meets at the Arts Centre. In October group members will read at the Arts Centre's Feel Good Fair to mark World Mental Health Day.

Bourne Ward is a secure psychiatric unit serving an area from Swindon to Bournemouth. Many of the people on the ward are too ill to work in a group or to use language in a coherent way, but as their illness becomes less acute they may join the writing groups which is run with an Occupational Therapist as part of her clinical activity. Notes are written up and detailed supervision takes place after each workshop. Much of the group's work is oral and results are displayed on the day room notice board.

Men's Words is a writing group for men attending the GP Surgery at Bemerton Heath, an area of social and economic deprivation on the outskirts of Salisbury. The group is small but committed, with members returning after periods of hospitalisation. In contrast, Amesbury Ward is a busy orthopaedic unit at Salisbury District Hospital. Fortnightly sessions consist of one-to-one oral work at bedsides. Where permission is given, this work is typed up and returned to the ward notice-board.

KickStart Poets are a poetry club who meet at Salisbury Arts Centre. Some of their members are interested in poetry and healing and the project offers them training days as well as the opportunity to sit in on workshops in order to deepen their experience of and interest in the field.

8 FURTHER READING

WHAT NEXT?

The recommendations which follow are just starting points. Among the great body of reading available to anyone interested in this field are the poetry of Emily Dickinson; Hopkins' 'Terrible Sonnets' and David Jones' 'In Parenthesis'; the later Hölderlin; Robert Lowell; Akmatova, Mandelstam and Tsvetaeva; Sylvia Plath in prose and poetry; Rainer Maria Rilke; any number of literary biographies and autobiographies; Proust; Marion Milner's memoirs or the philosophy of Martin Heidegger...

Writing and personal development

Some of these books offer encouragement and a structure as you work alone; others are designed to help writers leading groups. Still others have a writer reflecting on their experiences.

Gillie Bolton: *The Therapeutic Potential of Creative Writing: Writing Myself* (Jessica Kingsley, 1999)

Natalie Goldberg: *Writing Down the Bones* (Shambhala, 1986)

Celia Hunt and Fiona Sampson (eds.): *The Self on the Page: Theory and practice of creative writing and personal development*. (Jessica Kingsley, 1998)

Nicki Jackowska: *Write for Life* (Element 1997)

John Killick and Myra Schneider: *Writing for Self-Discovery* (Element 1997)

Barry Lane: *Writing as a Road to Self-Discovery* (Writers Digest, 1993)

David Morley: *Under the Rainbow: writers and artists in school* (Bloodaxe, 1991)

Louise DeSalvo: *Writing as a Way of Healing* (Women's Press, 1999)

Running a project

Lynne Alexander: *Now I Can Tell* (Macmillan, 1990)

– Stunning record of residency at a hospice.

The Arts Council Writer in Residence Guidelines (The Arts Council of England,1999)

– Essential reading on practitioners' rights!

British Association for Counselling, 1 Regent Place, Rugby CV21 2PJ for up-to-date Code of Ethics and Practice.

Malcolm Dickson (ed.): *Art with People* (AN Publications, 1995)

– A guide to the ethos and history of community arts activities, with useful Further Reading.

Fi Frances: *The Arts and Older People* (Age Concern, 1999)

– Comprehensive, clear and well-laid-out.

Duncan Haldane and Susan Loppert (eds.): *The Arts in Health Care: Learning from Experience* (King's Fund, 1999)

– Includes a chapter by Dr Robin Philipp on evaluating uses of creative writing in mental health care.

Charles Kaye and Tony Blee (eds.) *The Arts in Health Care: A Palette of Possibilities* (Jessica Kingsley, 1997)

– Looks at projects across the art forms.

National Association of Writers in Education *Writing in Education.*

– Magazine with frequent articles by poetry and healing practitioners.

Malcolm Rigler: *Withymoor Village Surgery – A Health Hive* (Withymoor Village Surgery, 1997)

– See Section Three.

Peter Senior and Jonathan Croall: *Helping to Heal: The Role of the Arts in Health Care* (Calouste Gulbenkian Foundation, 1993)

– Lays out some of the original arguments.

Tamara Smith *Live Literature* (The Arts Council of England, 1999)

– Full of practical advice and promotional ideas.

Contemporary poetry (and some prose)

This personal and very partial list includes further reading from featured poets but excludes books mentioned in other sections of the guide.

Chris Agee: *Scar on the Stone: Contemporary poetry from Bosnia* (Bloodaxe, 1998)

Jack Clemo: *Approach to Murano* (Bloodaxe, 1993)

– Visionary poet who's both deaf and blind.

Carol Ann Duffy (ed.): *Stopping for Death: poems of death and loss* (Viking, 1996)

Sara Dunn, Blake Morrison and Michèle Roberts (eds.) *Mindreadings: Writers' Journeys Through Mental States* (Minerva, 1996).

Barbara Charlesworth Gelpi and Albert Gelpi: *Adrienne Rich's Poetry and Prose* (Norton Critical Editions, 1993)

Menna Elfyn: *Cell Angel* (Bloodaxe, 1996)

– The political search for an identity in language.

Selima Hill: *A Little Book of Meat* (Bloodaxe, 1993); *Trembling Hearts in the Bodies of Dogs* (Bloodaxe, 1994)

Ted Hughes: *Tales from Ovid* (Faber, 1997)

Jaan Kaplinski: *Through the Forest* (Harvill, 1996)

Jack Mapanje: *The Chattering Wagtails of Mikuyu Prison* (Heinemann, 1993)

Les Murray: *Fredy Neptune* (Carcanet, 1998)

Ken Smith: *Wormwood* (Bloodaxe, 1987).

– Written while poet in residence in Wormwood Scrubs.

Pauline Stainer: *The Ice-Pilot Speaks* (Bloodaxe, 1994)

Eira Stenberg: *Wings of Hope and Daring* (Bloodaxe, 1992)

R. S. Thomas: *No Truce with the Furies* (Bloodaxe, 1995)